AF228279

SAVING THE ASIAN ELEPHANT

LOUISE SPILSBURY

CHERITON
CHILDREN'S BOOKS

Published in 2023 by **Cheriton Children's Books**
PO Box 7258, Bridgnorth WV16 9ET, UK

First Edition

Author: Louise Spilsbury
Designer: Paul Myerscough
Editor: Jane Brooke
Proofreader: Tracey Kelly
Consultant: David Hawksett, BSc

Printed in China

Publisher's Note: The information in the Kids on a Mission features in this book are suggestions for actions that children can take to help protect endangered animals, based on extensive research by the author and consultant. The email addresses and the children featured in the photographs are for illustrative purposes only.

Please visit our website,
www.cheritonchildrensbooks.com,
to see more of our high-quality books.

CONTENTS

ASIAN ELEPHANTS IN DANGER

Elephants are the largest land-living animals in the world. Elephants look like no other animal on our planet. They have huge bodies, long trunks, and big tusks. Sadly, these gentle giants are in serious danger. And the biggest threats they face are from humans.

ELEPHANTS UNDER THREAT

At the beginning of the twentieth century, there were probably more than 100,000 Asian elephants on Earth. Today, fewer than 50,000 can still be found in the wild. In just over 100 years, the number of Asian elephants on the planet has halved. Elephants have been hunted in huge numbers by humans. They have been killed for their tusks and skin. Their homes have also been destroyed because of human activity. People are cutting down the forests where Asian elephants live. They are doing so to make room for homes, farms, roads, and industries.

▲ Young or weak elephants are at risk from lions, tigers, or crocodiles. However, adult Asian elephants are too big and strong for most **predators** to kill. Adult Asian elephants are only in danger from humans.

"The elephant can survive only if forests survive."

Mark Shand, travel writer and **conservationist**

NO MORE ELEPHANTS

Asian elephants are even more **endangered** than their African cousins. Conservationists are warning us that we need to do more to save the remaining Asian elephants on Earth. If we do not, one day these intelligent animals may be gone forever.

HELP THE ASIAN ELEPHANT!

There is still hope for the Asian elephant, and it is not too late to save it. People everywhere have heard the Asian elephant's trumpet for help. And they are making it their mission to help these amazing animals survive. In this book, we'll learn about the Asian elephant and why it is in danger. We'll discover what people are doing to help Asian elephants and how they have built a career in **conservation**. We'll find out how kids everywhere can make it their mission to help save the Asian elephant. And we'll learn how you can make a career in conservation your mission. Feeling mission-ready? Then read on!

The International Union for Conservation of Nature (IUCN) keeps a record of the world's **species** and how at risk of **extinction** they are. It is called the

Red List.

There are more than

142,500

species on the Red List.

The Asian elephant is listed as

endangered.

CHAPTER ONE

MEET THE ASIAN ELEPHANT

Asian elephants are amazing creatures. They are not quite as large as African elephants, but they are still high and mighty. When fully grown, these huge beasts can weigh up to 1,100 pounds (4,989 kg). They can grow up to 11.5 feet (3.5 m) tall and around 21 feet (around 6 m) long.

ELEPHANT SPEAK

Elephants make different sounds. They can rumble, trumpet, and roar. Trumpeting is created by pushing air through the trunk. Elephants use sounds to tell other elephants they are excited, angry, or in danger. The sounds carry for distances of up to 10 miles (16 km).

KEEPING COOL

An elephant's huge ears have an important job to do. They help keep the animal cool. The ears contain many **blood vessels**. When an elephant flaps its ears, the blood in the veins cools. That in turn cools the elephant's brain. The cooled blood then travels through the body. That helps reduce the animal's body temperature by several degrees.

SPECIAL TEETH

Tusks are special, long front teeth. Both male and female African elephants can have tusks. However, only some male Asian elephants have tusks. The tusks are made of **ivory**. They are **incisor** teeth used for digging and uprooting trees. They are also put on display, for people to show off to others. The tusks keep on growing throughout an elephant's life. A tusk can grow as fast as 1 inch (2.5 cm) per year.

SUPER-STRONG TRUNKS

An elephant's trunk is made up of a very long upper lip and nose. Elephant trunks have 100,000 muscles! They are so strong that they can push over a tree. Each trunk has a pointed part known as a finger. The elephant uses it to grip and pick up delicate objects, such as peanuts.

In a Group

Scientists group animals to help them classify, or order, them. Asian elephants belong to a group of animals called *Elephas maximus*. An Indian elephant is one type of Asian elephant.

WHERE ASIAN ELEPHANTS LIVE

Asian elephants once roamed freely across most of Asia. Today, Asian elephants are found in just 15 percent of the **territory** in which they once lived. They are found in 13 countries in South and Southeast Asia. Their territory stretches from India in the west and Nepal in the north, to Sumatra in the south and Borneo in the east. Asian elephants live in forest **habitats**. They also live in **grassland** or scrubland areas between the forests. Elephants need to drink at least once a day, so Asian elephants are always found close to a source of fresh water.

TYPES OF ASIAN ELEPHANT

There are four different types or **subspecies** of Asian elephants.

- There are more Indian elephants (*Elephas maximus indicus*) than any other types of Asian elephants. There are between 20,000 and 25,000 of them.
- The Bornean elephant (*Elephas maximus borneensis*) is the smallest. There are fewer than 1,500 left in the wild.
- Sumatran elephants (*Elephas maximus sumatranus*) are **critically endangered**. There are only 2,400 to 2,800 left in the wild.
- The Sri Lankan elephant (*Elephas maximus maximus*) is the largest and darkest of the Asian elephants. There are 2,500 to 4,000 of these animals left in the wild.

▲ Bornean elephants have very long tails. They also have large ears and straighter tusks when compared with other Asian elephants.

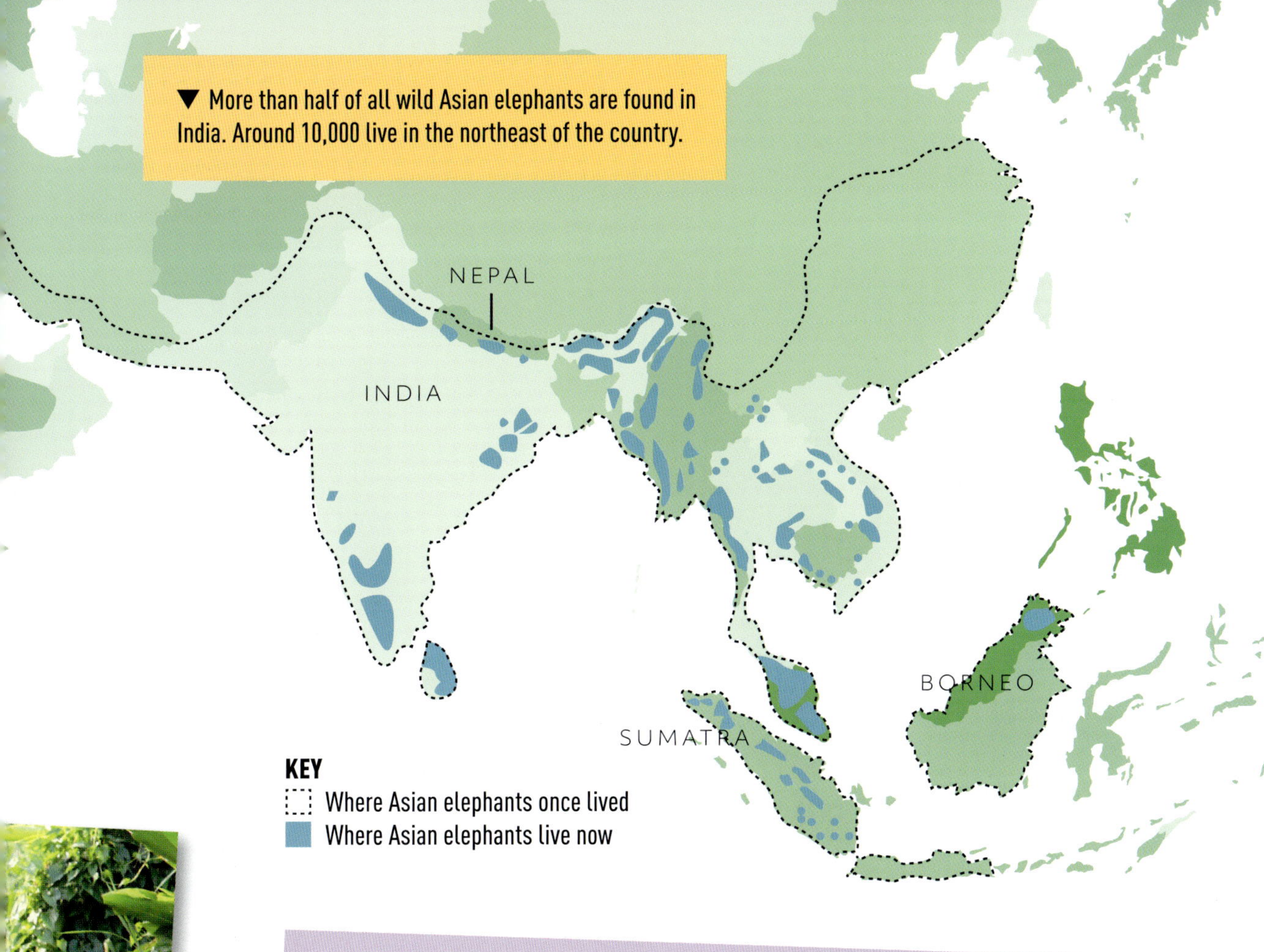

▼ More than half of all wild Asian elephants are found in India. Around 10,000 live in the northeast of the country.

BIG ANIMALS, BIG HOMES

Elephants are big animals, and they need big spaces in which to live. A **home range** is the area covered every year by a wild animal in its natural habitat. Female Asian elephants live in groups with their female relatives and their young, while males usually live alone. Males have bigger home ranges, but both males and females need a lot of room to wander. They eat and drink vast amounts of food and water, so they need a large area to provide them with all they need to survive. Elephants do not walk far in one day, but their total home range can be more than 200 square miles (517 sq km).

WHY SHOULD WE HELP THE ASIAN ELEPHANT?

Asian elephants are incredibly important to the **environments** in which they live. Without these greedy guzzlers, the forests in which they roam would suffer. That would affect not only the elephants, but other wildlife and people in the area, too.

FORESTS NEED ELEPHANTS

Asian elephants keep forests healthy. They eat huge amounts of plants and fruit. They leave 15 to 20 different **dung** piles across their home range every day. The seeds from the fruits they eat pass through the elephant's digestive system. They leave it in the dung, whole and undamaged. The dung also acts as a **fertilizer** to help those seeds grow in the dirt. The seeds grow into new trees.

SHAPING THE FOREST

Asian elephants help shape the forests in other ways, too. Elephants knock down trees to reach the fruits that grow on their branches. They also clear pathways through forests as they travel. That creates gaps in the treetops that let in sunlight. The sunlight helps young plants grow. That keeps the forests healthy. When elephants cannot find a stream or river, they dig for water beneath Earth's surface. The water that then bubbles to the surface provides other animals with drinking water, too.

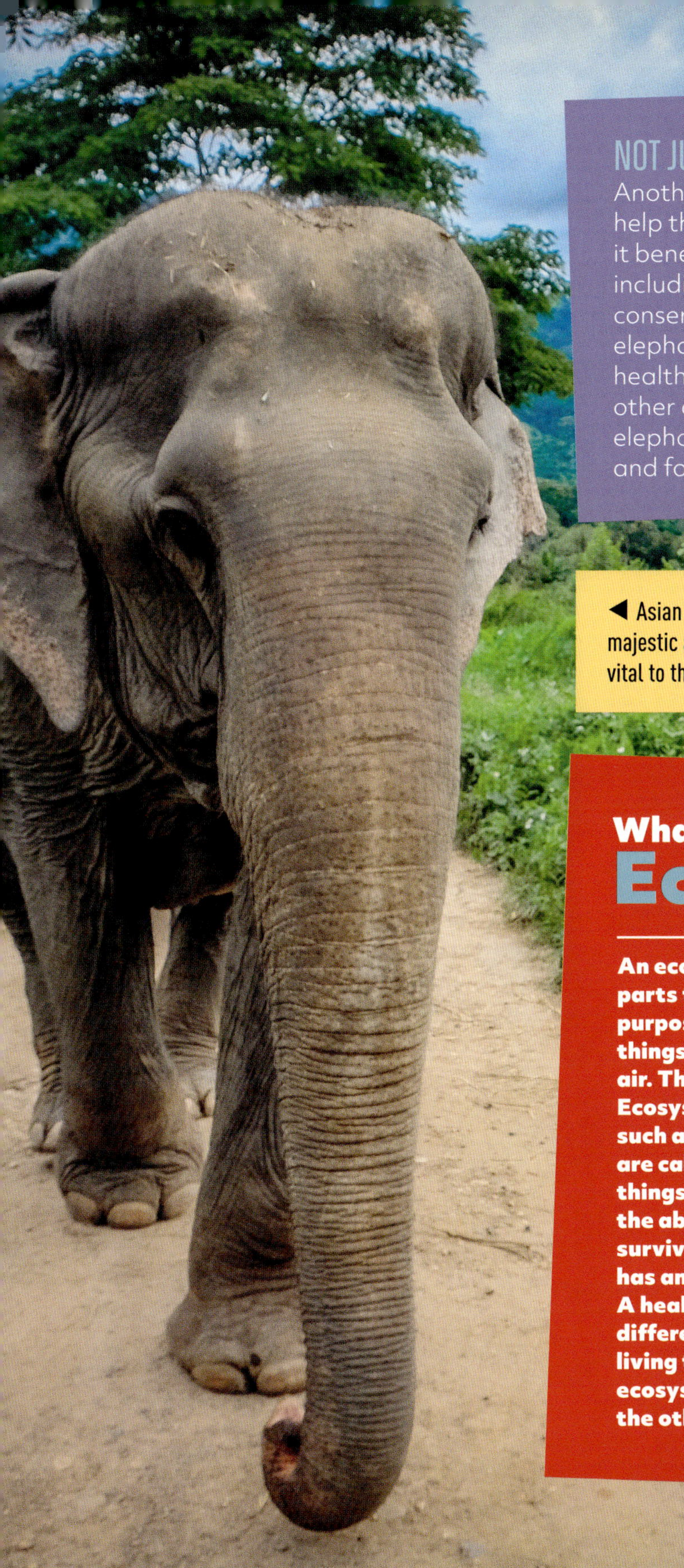

What Is an
Ecosystem?

An ecosystem is a group of natural parts that all work together for a purpose. Ecosystems include nonliving things such as water, sunshine, and air. These are called abiotic factors. Ecosystems also include living things such as plants and animals. These are called biotic factors. The living things in an ecosystem depend on the abiotic factors in the ecosystem to survive. Every part of the ecosystem has an important part to play. A healthy ecosystem has many different plants and animals living together. If any part of that ecosystem changes or is damaged, the other parts are affected, too.

ASIAN ELEPHANTS LIKE TO EAT!

Asian elephants love to eat! In fact, they spend more than three-quarters of each day eating. They feast on grasses, tree bark, and roots. They also eat leaves, fruit, and small stems. Elephants eat around 330 pounds (150 kg) of plant foods each day.

TREE TREATS

Elephants use their trunks to gather food. They use their long trunks to reach the tops of trees, where leaves and fruits grow. They also use their trunks to shake trees. That makes their fruits and nuts fall to the ground. Elephants also bend trees or snap off branches to reach leaves and fruit.

NEW TEETH

Elephant teeth work hard to chew all the **fibrous** plant food they eat. Asian elephants grow six sets of small teeth over a lifetime. As the front rows of teeth wear out, they break and fall out. Then a new set of teeth move forward, like a conveyor belt!

DIRT-FREE FEEDING

When an Asian elephant pulls up a clump of grass to eat, it doesn't swallow the dirt attached. It washes off the dirt by moving the grass back and forth in water. It then eats the grass.

KEEPING HEALTHY

Elephants use their tusks to strip bark off trees. They also use their tusks to scrape soil or rock off surfaces. Elephants eat soil and rock. That is because they contain important **minerals** they need to keep healthy, such as salt. Elephants cannot get those minerals from the plant materials they eat.

PEOPLE ON A MISSION

Many people are fighting to save Asian elephants. Some work in conservation. They have made it their mission to devote their career to protecting elephants. They want to ensure that these huge animals are still parading through the forests in the future.

PEOPLE IN OFFICES

Some conservationists work in elephant forest habitats in Asia. It is their job to keep a watchful eye on the elephants in their areas. They may perform tasks such as counting the number of elephants in an area. They keep a check on the health of the forests in which the elephants live. They alert authorities if they see the forest being damaged. Some conservationists work closely with local people. They talk to them about how Asian elephants help keep the forests healthy for humans, too.

PEOPLE ON THE GROUND

Many conservationists work in the places where Asian elephants live in the wild. Wildlife managers and officers help protect the Asian elephant's habitat and monitor its numbers. Wildlife technicians collect information on Asian elephants and their habitats, and they often work alongside a wildlife manager. Public educators and outreach specialists work with people to help educate them about Asian elephants. They encourage people to protect Asian elephants and help the conservationists keep the animals' habitats safe.

PEOPLE EVERYWHERE

Many ordinary people around the world are doing what they can to help Asian elephants. They are raising money to support projects and people that are protecting Asian elephants. They are trying to teach others about the threats Asian elephants face. They are joining organizations that help Asian elephants. They are changing their lifestyles to protect the precious Asian elephants, too.

MAKE IT YOUR MISSION

You can help Asian elephants and other endangered animals by taking action and planning a career in conservation. Here's how:

1. In this book, you'll discover what actions kids on a mission can take to help Asian elephants. Use them to inspire your own actions to rescue Asian elephants.

2. You'll also discover some of the careers people on a mission have in Asian elephant conservation. As you read about each one, think about whether that career in conservation might suit you.

3. At the end of this book, you'll find a guide to how to build a career in conservation. Check it out to discover how you can make saving animals your life mission.

▲ Conservationists study habitats, including the plants that grow there, to learn more about species.

CHAPTER TWO

HOMES UNDER THREAT

The biggest threat to Asian elephants is habitat loss. Their forest homes have been destroyed at a disastrous rate. How did this happen?

PEOPLE MOVING IN

There are more people living in Asia than in any other **continent** on Earth, and the **population** is still growing. In fact, around 20 percent of the world's population live near Asian elephants. Increasing numbers of people all need somewhere to live and food to eat. As the population grows, people clear more of the forests in which Asian elephants live. They clear them to make way for towns, villages, and farms. People also build new roads and railroad lines that cut through Asian elephant territory.

TAKING OVER THE FORESTS

People are also **logging** forests to use the trees for timber. Timber is wood that people can use to make products such as furniture. Forests are also cleared to make space for **plantations** of plants and trees. The plantations produce rubber, tea, palm oil, and other resources. They are sold all over the world. Mining companies also clear forests. They dig into the land and collect coal and other resources. Power companies destroy trees to make space to build **hydropower** stations. Huge areas of land are being destroyed as a result.

ELEPHANT SAFE ZONES

One way to save Asian elephants is to protect their forests. Some conservationists are working to create wildlife reserves for Asian elephants. These are areas of land where people are not allowed to hunt or cut down trees and grasses. They also cannot graze farm animals, dig **mines**, or clear land for other industries on the land. Conservationists work hard to persuade governments to create elephant reserves.

◄ Asian elephants and humans are fighting for space. It is a battle that the elephants are losing.

"We need... solutions that help both elephants and people."

Dr. Barney Long, Asian species expert, the World Wildlife Fund (WWF)

Farms and plantations spell danger for Asian elephants. When forests are cleared to grow food, the elephants are pushed into increasingly smaller areas. There is not enough food in those areas to feed all of the elephants there. When elephants have less to eat, they become weak. They may have fewer babies. They may even starve to death.

HUNGRY ELEPHANTS

Hungry elephants may enter the farms and plantations that surround them to find food. They also charge into villages and break into people's homes, to steal food from kitchens and cupboards. Elephants are very strong and can cause a lot of damage. Local people get upset and angry when the damage elephants cause means they have no food to feed their families. They may hurt or kill the elephants to keep them from taking their food.

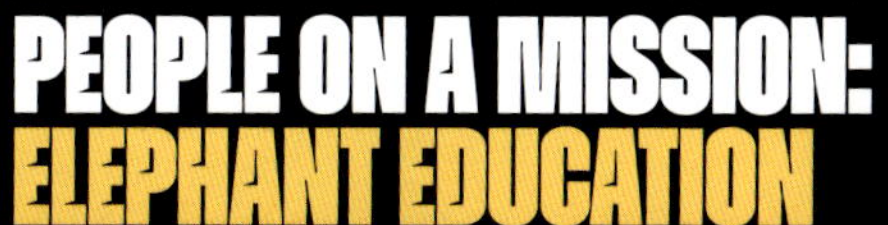

Public education and outreach specialists work with local people to educate them about Asian elephants. They explain the importance of protecting the animals and their habitats.

Specialists work with local communities to try and stop **conflicts** between them and the Asian elephants. They help them find ways to reduce conflict. For example, they put up signs to warn people not to leave fruit in their cars or feed the elephants. Specialists work with governments and organizations to try and pay local people for any food they lose to elephants.

Specialists also encourage farmers and villagers to use easy solutions to protect their crops and food supplies. They suggest that villagers plant lemon trees around their homes. Elephants do not like lemon trees, so planting them helps reduce human–elephant conflict. Specialists show people how to build concrete walls or dig deep trenches around farms. By using those methods, people can reduce the risk of elephant raids.

Specialists and organizations employ locals to patrol villages. For example, they may be employed as park rangers. It is their job to keep elephants from entering villages. The rangers use firecrackers or trucks to steer the elephants back into the forest.

◀ For farmers, elephant raids can be costly. Sometimes, they are hurt or even killed when they try to chase hungry elephants away from their farms.

When a small herd of elephants ▶ raids a small farm, they may eat all the crops in one night. That can be disastrous for a poor farming family.

SHARING ITS HOME

The Asian elephant is not the only animal threatened by habitat destruction. **Deforestation** is causing some other amazing animals in Southeast Asia to become endangered, too.

GREATER ONE-HORNED RHINO

The Mogul emperors ruled parts of South Asia from the early sixteenth century until the mid-eighteenth century. They once used greater one-horned rhinos in fights against elephants as entertainment. Thankfully, that no longer happens. However, the rhinos are still under threat. Hunters kill them for their single horns. The animals are also affected by habitat loss.

THE MALAYAN TAPIR

Malayan tapirs are unusual-looking animals. They eat plant parts and fruits from the forest floor. They have long, fleshy noses. Tapirs have lived on Earth for at least 50 million years. Tapirs are threatened by habitat loss and hunting, just like the Asian elephant.

THE ORANGUTAN

Orangutans share the rain forests of Sumatra with Asian elephants. The great ape is at home high up in the treetops. The name *orangutan* means "person of the forest." These striking animals are covered in shaggy red fur. Like Asian elephants, orangutans are also endangered and in need of human help.

THE TIGER

Today, most tigers live in India and Thailand. Sadly, these beautiful, fierce animals are losing their habitats. They are also being killed for their fur and bones. Since the beginning of the twentieth century, the number of wild tigers in the world has dropped by more than 95 percent. Today, there are only around 3,900 tigers left in the wild.

CHAPTER THREE

UNDER THREAT FROM HUNTING

Hunting and killing Asian elephants is a crime. Unfortunately, it still happens. Poaching is the illegal killing or capture of animals. Poachers hunt and kill Asian elephants. They sell their ivory tusks and other body parts for a lot of money.

TUSKS FOR SALE

Most ivory tusks come from poaching African elephants. However, Asian elephants are also illegally hunted for their ivory. In Asian elephants, only the males grow tusks. That is why poachers mainly target male elephants. The ivory tusks are made into items that are sold to tourists in souvenir stores in Asia. They are also exported, or sold abroad. Today, ivory is carved into objects. They include statues, chopsticks, pipes, and combs. Ivory is also made into other goods.

HIGH-VALUE HIDES

Other Asian elephant body parts have great value to poachers, too. Poachers kill male and female elephants for their hides, or skins. Some of them are dried and turned to powder. It is used in medicines that people mistakenly believe can cure stomach problems. Dried elephant skin is also made into jewelry. It is turned into luxury leather goods, too. They include designer bags, boots, wallets, belts, and motorcycle seats.

Xu Ling, head of WWF-China's wildlife **trade** program

BREAKING THE LAW

There are laws in place to keep people from buying and selling certain wild plants and animals. The problem is that people can earn huge amounts of money from wildlife crime. For that reason, some people are willing to risk being caught. The crimes they commit are having a serious impact on elephant populations.

▲ The illegal wildlife trade is a secretive business, so it is impossible to know exactly how much money is made from the trade in Asian elephant parts.

POACHING

Poaching for ivory took place throughout the twentieth century. Most hunters used spears or cheap guns to kill elephants. At that time, ivory was used to produce ornaments and small carvings. It was also used for items such as piano keys and chess sets. The number of elephants killed increased dramatically during the 1970s and 1980s. That is when poachers started to use more powerful guns. During that time, around 100,000 elephants were poached every year. A ban on poaching ivory began in 1989. However, it has not stopped hunters from poaching Asian elephants.

▼ Elephant tusks are worth a lot of money to poachers. For that reason, poachers risk entering protected **reserves** to hunt elephants.

CRUEL KILLING

Poachers usually kill elephants before removing the tusks. However, sometimes the elephants don't die immediately. Elephants feel an enormous amount of pain when their tusks are cut off. If the elephant isn't dead when its tusks are removed, it dies soon afterward. It dies from wound infection. Elephant poaching is incredibly cruel.

PEOPLE ON A MISSION: ELEPHANT PROTECTORS

Wildlife officers are conservation workers whose job it is to protect Asian elephants from poaching and other threats. Wildlife officers patrol the areas for which they are responsible for days at a time. They check on the Asian elephants that live there. They may even have to find their food while on patrol. They may look for fruit or catch fish. A search for poachers can take weeks.

Wildlife officers use technology to help them find poachers. They fly **drones** with cameras over elephant habitats. Drones help them locate poachers. They also help them monitor elephant numbers and movements. Officers also set up surveillance and thermal-imaging cameras. They place them near **watering holes** and other places where poachers might target Asian elephants. They also use low-tech solutions such as sniffer dogs to find poachers. The dogs are trained to smell poachers. They are also trained to smell illegal wildlife products, even if they have been put into containers for export.

Wildlife officers often wait until night to arrest poachers, when they are asleep. They can then catch them unawares. In some places, poachers face the death penalty for killing an elephant. The death penalty is punishment by death. For that reason, poachers will do anything to escape arrest. That includes hurting or killing wildlife officers. Many officers have lost their lives trying to protect Asian elephants.

These elephant tusks were ▶ taken from poachers in Sri Lanka. It became the first South Asian country to destroy poached ivory.

CALVES NEED THEIR MOMS

The poaching of Asian elephants poses a real threat to the species. When female elephants are killed for their hide, or skin, the calves, or babies, in the herd may die. Elephant babies rely on their mother and other female elephants for their survival.

HERE COMES BABY!

When it's time for a female elephant to give birth, the other female elephants in the herd surround her. They kick up a circle of dust and dirt. They do so to protect her from predators. Females are vulnerable when they give birth.

STARTING OUT

An Asian elephant mother gives birth while standing. She usually has just one calf. Twins are rare. A newborn calf is helped to its feet by its mother and other females. The calf can stand on its own within minutes of being born.

FEEDING TIME

A calf stands soon after birth, so it can nurse. That means the mother feeds the baby with milk from her body. Calves drink a lot! They drink more than 17.5 pints (10 L) of milk each day for their first year of life. After that, they start to eat plants, too. However, they continue to nurse for three years.

BABYSITTING CLUB

The entire herd of females protects the calf. If a predator approaches, they surround the calf. When the calf's mother is busy, young female elephants babysit! Other females in the herd can even nurse the calf.

LEARNING TO LIVE

Elephant calves learn everything from their herd. They learn which plants are safe to eat. They discover where to find water. They learn how to behave. An elephant mother uses her trunk to coax or steer her calf along. She also slaps the calf if it is naughty! She strokes and cuddles it with her trunk, too.

CLIMATE CHANGE THREATS

Climate change is one of the biggest problems facing Earth. Climate change doesn't affect only humans. It also threatens Asian elephants and other animals. As Earth's temperature increases, our world is experiencing big changes in weather patterns. That affects us all.

WHAT IS CLIMATE CHANGE?

Climate change describes the average weather conditions in a region over a long period of time. Earth's climate has changed slowly for the entire history of our planet. These changes were due to natural causes such as changes in the sun and **geological** activity. The difference with the climate change that is happening now is that it is caused by human activities. These include burning **fossil fuels**, which releases gases into Earth's **atmosphere**. These gases, known as greenhouse gases, surround the planet like a blanket, causing Earth to heat up. Changes in temperature in Earth's atmosphere affect the planet's weather patterns in different ways.

"This change (climate change) is forcing elephants to barge into the farms on the lookout for food."

Tensing Bodosa, Indian tea farmer

FLOODS AND DROUGHTS

Each year, South Asia experiences a summer **monsoon** season. It usually begins in May, when monsoon winds bring heavy rain. The rains provide relief from a long, dry season. They continue for a few months, watering plants and filling water sources. The problem is that climate change is causing more extreme monsoon patterns. Sometimes, less rain falls, or it falls for only a short amount of time. That causes drought, which is a period of time with little or no rain. Sometimes, huge amounts of rain fall in a short amount of time. That causes floods, occasions when large amounts of water cover otherwise normally dry land. Droughts kill plants, and floodwaters can rip away plants and trees. Elephants rely on those trees and other plants for food.

◄ As the areas of water that elephants rely on dry up, these animals are being placed in even greater danger.

▼ Burning fossil fuels is disastrous for the natural world. Its contribution to climate change is damaging the future of wildlife.

Kids on a Mission

@jen-ellie-2008

I am helping to plant new trees. More plants and trees will help remove the greenhouse gas **carbon dioxide (CO2)** from the air.

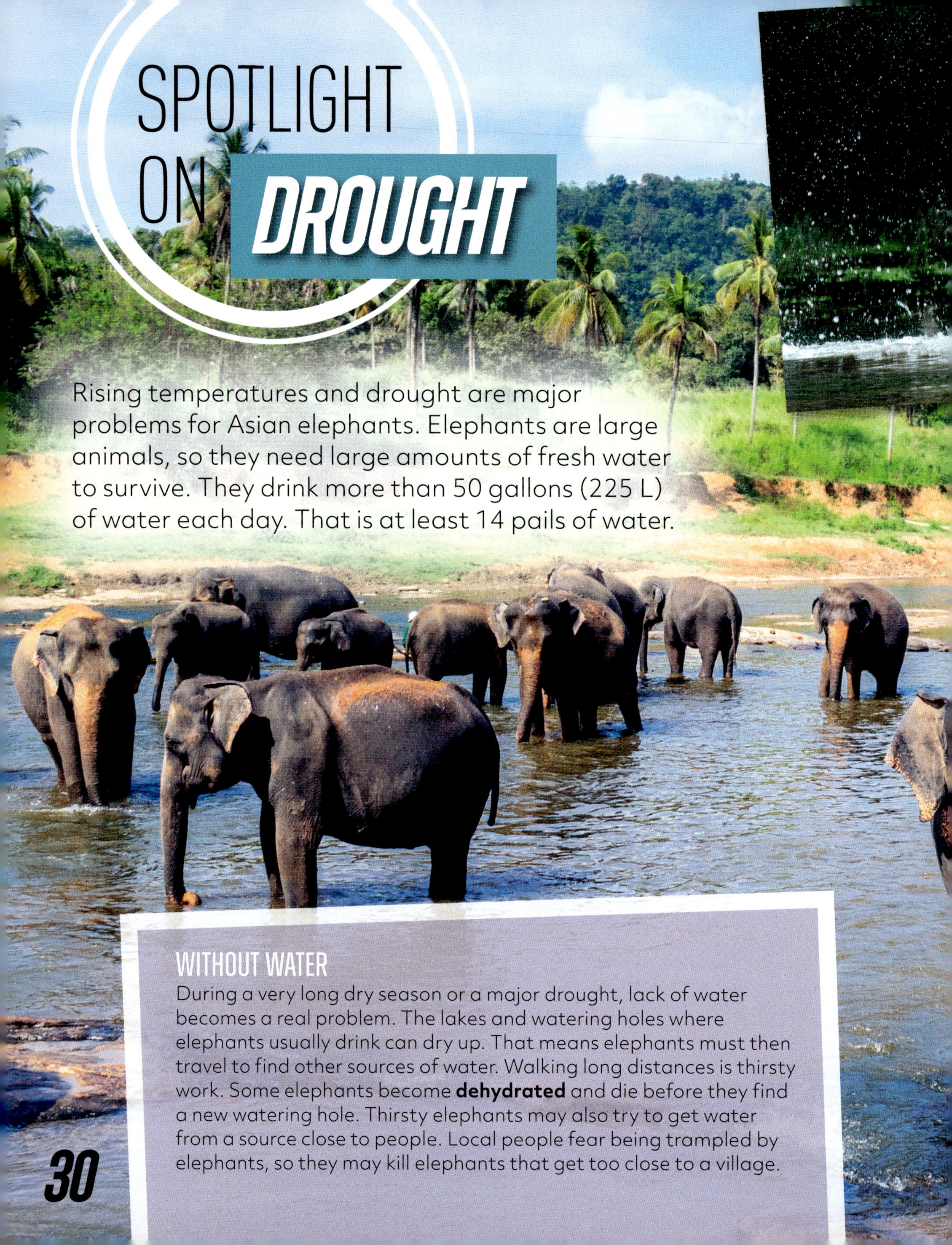

SPOTLIGHT ON DROUGHT

Rising temperatures and drought are major problems for Asian elephants. Elephants are large animals, so they need large amounts of fresh water to survive. They drink more than 50 gallons (225 L) of water each day. That is at least 14 pails of water.

WITHOUT WATER

During a very long dry season or a major drought, lack of water becomes a real problem. The lakes and watering holes where elephants usually drink can dry up. That means elephants must then travel to find other sources of water. Walking long distances is thirsty work. Some elephants become **dehydrated** and die before they find a new watering hole. Thirsty elephants may also try to get water from a source close to people. Local people fear being trampled by elephants, so they may kill elephants that get too close to a village.

PEOPLE ON A MISSION:
BATTLING CLIMATE CHANGE

Many people are helping Asian elephants by studying climate change and finding ways to prevent it from getting worse. They work in important environmental careers.

Climate and environmental scientists conduct research on climate change. They study how climate change affects different habitats and the animals that live within them. For example, some scientists are making **computer models**. They show how climate change will affect the Asian elephant's habitat and dry up water sources there. Scientists look at places where elephants might live in the future. They include mountains, where it is cooler and there is more water.

Campaigners raise awareness of climate change and the effect it is having on Asian elephants and other wildlife. They work in organizations such as charities. They create and run campaigns. The campaigns alert governments, other organizations, and people everywhere about the dangers of climate change.

Conservationists are finding ways to secure fresh water for elephants in the future. That could mean creating climate refuges. They are areas with water supplies that could be set aside for elephants. Alongside that work, it is important to make sure there are separate water sources for people and their farm animals. That will reduce conflict with elephants over water.

Drought and rising temperatures will make it more and more difficult for elephants to get the water they need.

MAKING A SPLASH!

Asian elephants love water. They also love muddy pools. They usually live close to a lake, pond, or river. They need water to drink. They also cool down in it. In the water, they enjoy rolling around and splashing. They even play-fight with the other members of their herd. Elephants are also strong swimmers.

KEEPING COOL

Elephants can die if they get too hot. When temperatures rise, elephants use water to cool off. They suck up water in their trunks and then spray it all over themselves.

DRINK UP!

Asian elephants do not drink with their trunks. Instead, they fill them with water. They then pour the water into their mouths.

MUD BATH!

Elephants also cool off by taking a mud bath. They love wallowing in pools of mud on a sunny day. As they roll around, they can often be heard trumpeting and roaring for joy!

GOING SNORKELING

Elephants can use their trunks like snorkels. In deep water, they use their trunks to breathe. In some places, elephants can even swim from island to island using this method.

MUD MASKS

After a bath in the water or mud, Asian elephants use their trunks to cover themselves with a layer of dirt and mud. It acts as both a sunscreen and bug spray!

CHAPTER FIVE

OTHER THREATS TO ASIAN ELEPHANTS

Habitat loss, hunting, and climate change are major threats to Asian elephants. However, these fascinating animals also face other dangers.

PUT TO WORK

Around 4,000 years ago, people began to capture Asian elephants. They trained them to work for them. Ever since, people in Asia have used elephants to carry timber, transport crops, and do other heavy work. Machines such as tractors are used today, but Asian elephants still do a lot of heavy lifting. Elephants are also kept in **captivity** to entertain tourists. They provide rides or perform in circuses. Unfortunately, most Asian elephants taken from the wild and used in these ways are neither healthy nor happy.

@ecowarrior_2007

I'm finding out more about elephants being trained to entertain tourists. I've told my friends to learn more too. If we all get involved, we can do more to help the elephants.

A CRUEL LIFE

Capturing elephants for the timber industry and wildlife trade is illegal in many countries. They include India, Vietnam, and Myanmar. Despite that, the capture of elephants still happens. Most elephants used by circuses and for the tourist industry were captured in the wild. They were forced to leave their freedom and families behind. When baby elephants are snatched from their families, the mothers may be killed in front of the babies. They are then taken far away and kept chained and locked up. They are brought out only for training. That often involves being beaten until they learn to perform tricks for people's amusement. The animals often get sick. They may be put to sleep, because they turn on and attack the people who hurt them.

"The brutality to Asian elephants in tourism is often described as the worst animal cruelty of all."

Chris Packham, naturalist and television presenter

SPOTLIGHT ON CAPTIVITY

Some Asian elephants kept in captivity are found in zoos. There are benefits and disadvantages to keeping elephants in zoos. The disadvantage is that elephants kept in zoos often get sick. They live only around half as long as wild elephants. They can get bored and unhappy. However, zoo elephants are safe from poachers, habitat loss, and climate change.

ASIAN ELEPHANTS IN ZOOS

Many of the elephants we see in zoos today were born in captivity. They could not be safely released into the wild, because they would not survive. In good zoos, the animals are safe and cared for. Zookeepers make sure that the elephants keep moving. They have a variety of things to interest them in their **enclosures**, such as pools or hills and new toys. That stops the animals from becoming bored and keeps them fit. Also, education is an essential part of conservation. When people visit zoos and learn about the animals there, they are more likely to care about protecting wild populations and habitats.

▼ Baby elephants born in captivity can grow up without facing the dangers of the natural world.

PEOPLE ON A MISSION: ELEPHANT SCIENTISTS

Zoologists study Asian elephants in the wild and in zoos. They also conduct research in the lab, universities, and other organizations. Zoologists study Asian elephants to find out more about them and what diseases the animals suffer from. They learn how captivity affects Asian elephants.

Zoologists also work in wildlife reserves. There, they monitor changes in Asian elephant populations, and they study their behavior. They set up Asian elephant health programs to reduce risks of disease among the animals.

They ensure that vets know how to use equipment that can **diagnose** Asian elephant diseases. They make sure the vets know how to treat those diseases.

Scientists in labs work on new projects that could help Asian elephants. Scientists are developing an artificial, or human-made, version of natural ivory. They hope to create a material that looks and feels like ivory, but does not come from an elephant. If ivory carvers in countries such as China could use artificial ivory, there would be no need to poach elephants for their tusks.

37

OTHER ELEPHANTS IN DANGER

In Africa, two other types of elephants are in danger. They face similar challenges to the Asian elephant. They are threatened by habitat loss, climate change, and poaching.

THE AFRICAN SAVANNA ELEPHANT

African **savanna** elephants live in a variety of habitats in Africa, from savannas and forests to deserts. These huge animals grow 10–13 feet (3–4 m) tall and weigh 4–7 tons (3,630–6,350 kg). They have massive ears, and their front legs are longer than their back legs. Females and their young can live in groups of several hundred animals. They are led by a female. The males live alone. They spend most of their time feeding on grasses. However, they also eat a wide variety of other plants and fruits. With only 40,000–50,000 animals left in the wild, the species is classified as endangered.

THE AFRICAN FOREST ELEPHANT

African forest elephants live in the rain forests of west and central Africa. There, they are hidden among the thick forest trees. The animals are also very secretive. Therefore, the only way to figure out how many exist is by counting their dung piles! African forest elephants are 8–10 feet (2.4–3 m) tall and weigh 2–5 tons (1.8–4.5 mt), which is smaller than African savanna elephants. Their ears are more oval-shaped, and their tusks are straighter and point downward. African forest elephants live in family groups of up to 20 animals. They feed on leaves, grasses, and seeds. They also eat fruit and tree bark. They are critically endangered. Tens of thousands of them are killed each year for their ivory.

WHAT'S NEXT FOR THE ASIAN ELEPHANT?

Conservation efforts are making a real difference to the very serious threats that Asian elephants face. All over the world, ordinary people, conservationists, and governments are working to find solutions to the problems this magnificent animal faces. However, more needs to be done if Asian elephants really are going to have a chance of surviving into the future.

HELP FROM CONSERVATIONISTS

Asian elephants desperately need more conservationists working to help them. Those conservationists need to find solutions to many different problems. They include finding new ways to reduce human–elephant conflict—for example, by encouraging ethical tourism. That is when people visit and watch elephants that live in genuine sanctuaries. They are places that allow elephants to live in natural, big, open spaces. There, they live with other elephants, eat the correct food, and get proper healthcare when they need it. The elephants are also not expected to perform tricks for visitors.

@elephanthero_RI

I'm going to train to become a wildlife manager when I grow up. I want to do everything I can to help Asian elephants and other endangered animals.

Carmen Rademaker, The Asian Elephant Foundation (TAEF)

HELP FROM ORGANIZATIONS

The WWF is one organization fighting to save Asian elephants. It is working to increase the number and size of reserves and protected areas where elephants can safely live. The organization is battling to create more wildlife corridors. They are safe routes along which elephants can travel between reserves and protected areas. The WWF also works with environmental lawyers to improve laws that protect Asian elephants. For example, it campaigns for stronger laws to stop poaching and to ban the use of wild animals in circuses.

HELP FROM ALL OF US

Anyone and everyone can make a difference to the lives and future of Asian elephants. If we all raise awareness of the dangers of habitat loss and the illegal wildlife trade, we can help stop it. We can all try and live in more **sustainable** ways to reduce the threat of climate change. If we all join together, we can save the Asian elephant. It will mean that this intelligent and peaceful animal will be free to roam its forests and help keep those habitats healthy in the future.

MAKE IT YOUR MISSION: A CAREER IN CONSERVATION

If you care about the future of Asian elephants and other endangered animals, why not make protecting them your mission? You could do that by planning for a future career in conservation. There are descriptions of different conservation careers on pages 44–45. And here are things you can do right now to prepare for a career in conservation and help save Asian elephants.

▲ Wildlife protection organizations around the world are calling for better protection of elephants and other endangered animals. Why not join their fight?

START TODAY!

The job you get in the future could be affected by the grades you achieve now. Get ahead by working hard at school now. Focus in your science, English, and geography classes. Language classes could also prove useful. If you get a job overseas, being able to speak a foreign language will be very helpful.

GET INVOLVED

Join a conservation group or wildlife charity today. This is a great way to get in touch with other people who care about wildlife and learn more about what you can do to help endangered animals. By getting involved with charities and conservation organizations now, you will also prove to future employers that you have always been interested in conservation.

TAKE ACTION!

You have learned about some of the actions that help Asian elephants from the Kids on a Mission features in this book. Here are some more ideas for other activities that can help protect Asian elephants:

- Adopt an Asian elephant! Ask your parents to help you check out the WWF site for information about adopting Asian elephants.
- Never go to a park that advertises shows or unnatural elephant behavior, such as doing tricks or painting. Never ride an elephant or join a swimming session with elephants.
- Ask your school to hold a fundraising event to raise money for an organization such as WWF, so you can help them protect Asian elephants.
- Start a blog about Asian elephants and the dangers they face. Educate as many people as you can.
- Choose recycled tissue and toilet paper. These products are not made from paper from trees cut down in elephant forests.

GET EXPERIENCE

Work experience is valuable whatever career you choose. Getting work experience in wildlife conservation will help you find the best path for you in a future career. Work experience gives you the skills you need, too. Try volunteering at a local zoo or wildlife park, for a wildlife charity, or a conservation organization as soon as you are old enough.

Soon, the future of our planet ▶ will be in the hands of young people like you. Make it a brighter future!

43

CAREERS IN CONSERVATION

There are many different types of conservation careers. The one you choose depends on your specific areas of interest and your particular talents and skills. Here is information about some of them. You can find out about other conservation jobs on page 47 of this book.

▲ The work of an environmental scientist may involve monitoring the water quality in areas of important habitat.

ZOOLOGIST

A zoologist is a scientist who specializes in studying animals. In this role, you might study one species or a group of species. Zoolologists studying elephants conduct research to find out more about what the animals need to survive. This knowledge helps protect a species, and it helps manage how it adjusts to issues such as climate change.

WILDLIFE MANAGER

If you became a wildlife manager, you would work with wild animals and wild habitats. You would do a variety of jobs. They would include supervising hunting within an area and keeping track of the animal populations there. You would also make sure that the habitat is suitable for the animals in it. You might work with local people to encourage communities to help protect the animals. Most wildlife managers have a degree in environmental studies.

WILDLIFE TECHNICIAN

Wildlife technicians study wildlife in its natural habitat. They closely watch animal numbers and animal behavior. In this role you might work for resource companies, governments, and environmental firms. They help ensure that wildlife protection laws are followed. A degree in wildlife management is usually required for this role.

WILDLIFE ECONOMIST

Are you good at math? Some mathematicians work as wildlife economists. They assess ecosystems and figure out their value to people. They literally put a price on habitats and animals. That information can be used to persuade governments and companies to protect them.

POLICY AND ADVOCACY JOBS

If you are interested in law and like figuring out problems, you could help wildlife by working in a policy and advocacy conservation job. People who carry out this work help draft laws that protect wildlife. They also help develop important policies, or plans for action, to protect wildlife. They then advocate, or work to persuade governments or companies to take up the ideas. Good **communication** skills are needed.

ECOTOURISM JOBS

If you took up a career in ecotourism you would work with people and show them the natural world. You would do so in ways that are sustainable and do not negatively impact wildlife or habitats. Ecotourism is a very important part of conservation efforts in many countries, because it encourages people to care about the natural world. The money tourists pay also provides funds to protect habitats and animals.

◀ Working as a wildlife photographer or filmmaker are other interesting careers. They involve photographing or filming animals in their habitats as part of wildlife observation projects.

GLOSSARY

atmosphere the blanket of gases that surrounds Earth

blood vessels tubes in the body through which blood flows

brutality great violence

captivity kept in an enclosed space, not in the wild

carbon dioxide (CO2) a gas that contributes to climate change when released into the atmosphere

communication the sharing of messages or information

computer models predictions, based on data, that show what might happen

conflicts struggles or difficult encounters

conservation protection of the planet

conservationist a person who tries to protect the planet

continent one of Earth's seven major areas of land

critically endangered facing an extremely high risk of extinction in the wild

deforestation cutting down large areas of trees in a forest

dehydrated lacking the required amount of water in the body

diagnose to tell that a living thing has a disease or condition

drones unmanned flying vehicles that capture data as they travel

dung animal poop

enclosures spaces with walls or fencing in which animals are kept

endangered facing a very high risk of extinction in the wild

environments natural places where plants and animals live

extinction dying out

fertilizer a substance that helps plants grow

fibrous containing a lot of fiber, a substance in plants needed for healthy digestion

fossil fuels fuels formed from the remains of plants and animals that lived long ago

geological related to Earth's structure

grassland a large open area covered with grass and few trees

habitats places in which plants and animals live

home range an area over which an animal or group of animals regularly travels

hydropower the power of moving water

incisor one of four sharp front teeth

ivory the hard, white material that forms the tusks of elephants

logging cutting down trees

mammals warm-blooded animals that feed their young with milk from their bodies

minerals nutrients, or goodness, found in food that a body needs to be healthy

mines openings in the ground from which resources such as minerals are taken

monsoon a wind system of the Indian Ocean that blows from the southwest in summer and the northeast in winter

plantations areas on which crops such as coffee, sugar, and tea are grown

population all the members of a species living in a certain area

predators animals that hunt and eat other animals

reserves areas where wildlife can live in safety

resources things that people use

samples small amounts for testing

savanna a flat plain covered with grass and few trees

species a type of plant or animal

subspecies a subdivision of a plant or animal species that shows differences from others of the same species

sustainable can be relied upon for the forseeable future

territory an area of land that an animal regards as its own, which it may defend from other animals

trade the exchange of goods for money

watering holes areas of water from which animals drink

FIND OUT MORE

BOOKS

Bergin, Raymond. *Animals in Danger* (What on Earth? Climate Change Explained). Bearport Publishing, 2022.

Chodosh, Janie. *The Elephant Doctor of India*. Chicago Review Press, 2021.

Modany, Angela. *Animal Encyclopedia: 2,500 Animals with Photos, Maps, and More!* (National Geographic Kids). National Geographic Kids, 2021.

WEBSITES

Discover more about careers that help fight climate change at:
www.bestcolleges.com/blog/climate-change-jobs

Discover the ultimate guide to careers in conservation at:
www.conservation-careers.com/15-key-conservation-jobs-ultimate-guide-for-conservation-job-seekers

Hear directly from people working in conservation. Find out what they have to say about a career in conservation at:
www.conservation-careers.com/conservation-jobs-careers-advice/how-to-get-a-job-in-conservation

Find out more about Asian elephant conservation at:
www.fauna-flora.org/species/asian-elephant

Discover careers in environmental science at:
https://jobs.environmentalscience.org

Find lots of amazing wildlife careers and what they involve at this useful site:
www.thebalancecareers.com/careers-with-wildlife-125918

Discover what the world's leading wildlife organization, the WWF, is doing to help Asian elephants and how you can get involved:
www.worldwildlife.org/species/asian-elephant

Publisher's note to educators and parents:
All the websites featured above have been carefully reviewed to ensure that they are suitable for students. However, many websites change often, and we cannot guarantee that a site's future contents will continue to meet our high standards of educational value. Please be advised that students should be closely monitored whenever they access the Internet.

INDEX

ABOUT THE AUTHOR

Award-winning author Louise Spilsbury, who also writes under the name Louise Kay Stewart, has written more than 250 books for young people on a wide range of subjects. She especially loves writing about animals and learning more about what we can all do to protect amazing species such as the Asian elephant.

SAVING THE SNOW LEOPARD

LOUISE SPILSBURY

CHERITON
CHILDREN'S BOOKS

Published in 2023 by **Cheriton Children's Books**
PO Box 7258, Bridgnorth WV16 9ET, UK

© 2023 Cheriton Children's Books

First Edition

Author: Louise Spilsbury
Designer: Paul Myerscough
Editor: Jane Brooke
Proofreader: Tracey Kelly
Consultant: David Hawksett, BSc

Picture credits: Cover: Shutterstock/Warren Metcalf. Inside: p1: Shutterstock/Sergei Primakov; pp4-5: Shutterstock/Abeselom Zerit; pp6-7: Shutterstock/Abeselom Zerit; p7t: Shutterstock/Eric Isselee; p7l: Shutterstock/BearFotos; p7r: Shutterstock/Eric Isselee; p7b: Shutterstock/Eric Isselee; p9c: Shutterstock/Asmakhan992; pp: Shutterstock/Abeselom Zerit; pp: Shutterstock/Slowmotiongli; p12b: Shutterstock/Adalbert Dragon; p13b: Shutterstock/USBFCO; p13r: Shutterstock/Slowmotiongli; pp14-15: Shutterstock/Dr Ajay Kumar Singh; pp16-17: Shutterstock/Warren Metcalf; p17t: Shutterstock/Chatursunil; p17b: Shutterstock/Chatursunil; pp18-19: Shutterstock/Nora Yusuf; p19c: Shutterstock/Bildagentur Zoonar GmbH; pp20-21: Shutterstock/Wang LiQiang; p21t: Shutterstock/Mikhail Semenov; p21c: Shutterstock/Ondrej Prosicky; p21b: Shutterstock/Belovodchenko Anton; pp22-23: Shutterstock/Dennis W Donohue; p23t: Shutterstock/Africa Studio; p23b: Shutterstock/Africa Studio; pp24-25: Shutterstock/Sergei Primakov; pp26-27: Shutterstock/Ondrej Chvatal; p27t: Shutterstock/Bildagentur Zoonar GmbH; p27c: Shutterstock/Kwadrat; p27b: Shutterstock/Belizar; pp28-29: Shutterstock/Kwadrat; p29t: Shutterstock/NadyGinzburg; p29c: Shutterstock/Krakenimages.com; p29b: Shutterstock/Krakenimages.com; pp30-31: Shutterstock/Vincent Legrand; p30t: Shutterstock/Paul Gibbings; pp32-33: Shutterstock/Jim Cumming; p33t: Shutterstock/Dennis W Donohue; p33c: Shutterstock/Holly S Cannon; p33b: Shutterstock/Quincy Floyd; pp34-35: Shutterstock/SofotoCool; p35t: Shutterstock/Belizar; p35c: Shutterstock/Sergey Novikov; p35b: Shutterstock/Sergey Novikov; pp36-37: Shutterstock/Lauren Bilboe; p36b: Shutterstock/Andreas Rose; pp38-39: Shutterstock/Jo Reason; p38b: Shutterstock/Slowmotiongli; p39c: Shutterstock/The Len; p39b: Shutterstock/PhotocechCZ; pp40-41: Shutterstock/Kwadrat; p40c: Shutterstock/Pixelheadphoto Digitalskillet; p40b: Shutterstock/Pixelheadphoto Digitalskillet; p42t: Shutterstock/Vladimir Turkenich; p43b: Shutterstock/LeManna; p44t: Shutterstock/Panumas Yanuthai; p45b: Shutterstock/Chrisdorney.

Printed in the United States

Publisher's Note: The information in the Kids on a Mission features in this book are suggestions for actions that children can take to help protect endangered animals, based on extensive research by the author and consultant. The email addresses and the children featured in the photographs are for illustrative purposes only.

Please visit our website,
www.cheritonchildrensbooks.com,
to see more of our high-quality books.